Gracie
SHOOTING STRAIGHT FROM THE HEART

The C.R. Gibson Company, Norwalk, Connecticut 06856

Copyright © 1987 by Anne FitzGerald and Dorothy Hall
North American edition published by
The C.R. Gibson Company
Norwalk, Connecticut 06856
All rights reserved
Co-edition arranged with the help of Angus Hudson, London
Printed in Italy
ISBN 0-8378-1832-X

♡

Gracie

HAS A MESSAGE OF LOVE
JUST FOR YOU FROM
THE HEART OF YOUR
FATHER
IN
HEAVEN

ALWAYS REMEMBER···

PSALM 139:13

GOD CREATED YOU
··· AND YOU ARE
        WONDERFULLY MADE

··· AND HE ONLY MADE
            ONE OF YOU

I THESS . 4:9

GOD HIMSELF WILL
   TEACH YOU HOW TO LOVE

IMAGINE ··· LESSONS FROM
               THE MASTER

ROMANS 8:39

NOTHING WILL BE ABLE
TO SEPARATE YOU FROM
HIS LOVE IN JESUS

A PERFECT LOVE
        ... YOURS FOREVER

ROMANS 5:5

GOD HAS POURED
HIS LOVE INTO OUR HEARTS
BY HIS SPIRIT

...HIS LOVE
     HIS WONDERFUL LOVE

I John 4:12
<u>~~~~~~~~~~~</u>

WHEN WE LOVE ANOTHER
··· GOD'S LOVE IS MADE
        PERFECT IN US

 SO WHEN YOU LOVE
SOMEONE ··· TELL THEM!

I COR. 13:14
LOVE IS PATIENT
AND KIND

ALWAYS MAKE TIME
TO SHOW IT

EPHESIANS 5:2

... AND WALK IN LOVE
JUST AS CHRIST
LOVED YOU

ITS A PERFECT PATH
... IT DOESN'T GO ASTRAY

Col. 2:2

THAT THEIR HEARTS
MIGHT BE HAPPY, BEING
KNIT TOGETHER
          IN LOVE

YOU ARE PART OF HIS PATTERN!

1 COR. 13:8

LOVE NEVER FAILS

A RECIPE THAT CAN'T GO WRONG

I JOHN. 3:18

DON'T JUST LOVE IN
WORDS · · · SHOW IT IN
KIND DEEDS

SOMEBODY NEEDS YOU!

I COR. 14:1

PURSUE LOVE
... MAKE IT
YOUR AIM

REMEMBER
...PRACTICE MAKES
PERFE

PSALM 36:7

HOW PRECIOUS
IS YOUR STEADFAST LOVE
O GOD

NEVER FORGET IT
··· YOU ARE LOVED !

... JUST REMEMBER
        TO PASS
        IT ON!